OUR SOLAR SYSTEM

Venus

BY DANA MEACHEN RAU

Content Adviser: Dr. Stanley P. Jones, Assistant Director, Washington, D.C., Operations, NASA Classroom of the Future

Science Adviser: Terrence E. Young Jr., M.Ed., M.L.S., Jefferson Parish (La.) Public Schools

Reading Adviser: Dr. Linda D. Labbo, Department of Reading Education, College of Education, The University of Georgia

COMPASS POINT BOOKS

MINNEAPOLIS, MINNESOTA

For Mom

Compass Point Books
3722 West 50th Street, #115
Minneapolis, MN 55410

Visit Compass Point Books on the Internet at *www.compasspointbooks.com*
or e-mail your request to *custserv@compasspointbooks.com*

Photographs ©: NASA, cover, 1, 3, 5 (left), 12–13, 14, 16–17, 20–21; Scala/Art Resource, NY, 4; Stock Montage, 5 (right); North Wind Picture Archives, 6, 7; NASA/JPL/Caltech, 8–9, 15; Marilyn Moseley LaMantia/Graphicstock, 10, 26–27; Astronomical Society of the Pacific, 18, 22–23; NASA/NSSDC, 19; USGS, 24.

Editors: E. Russell Primm, Emily J. Dolbear, and Karen Commons
Photo Researchers: Svetlana Zhurkina and Jo Miller
Photo Selector: Karen Commons
Designer: The Design Lab
Illustrator: Graphicstock

Library of Congress Cataloging-in-Publication Data

Rau, Dana Meachen.
   Venus / by Dana Meachen Rau.
      p. cm. — (Our solar system)
   Includes bibliographical references and index.
   Summary: Describes the size, characteristics, and composition of the planet Venus.
   ISBN 0-7565-0201-2 (hardcover)
   1. Venus (Planet)—Juvenile literature. [1. Venus (Planet)] I. Title.
   QB621 .R38 2002
   523.42—dc21   2001004419

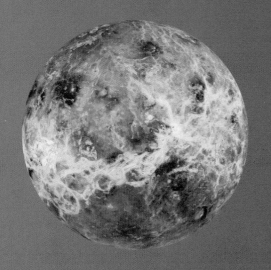

Table of Contents

Looking at Venus from Earth

Have you ever looked up into the night sky? You probably saw a lot of stars. One very bright point of light may have been a planet—Venus! Venus is one of the brightest objects in the sky. Only the Sun and the Moon are brighter.

People have been looking at Venus for thousands of years. Some people called Venus the "jewel of the sky." The Romans thought Venus looked very beautiful. They named it after Venus, their goddess of love and beauty. When it is seen in

The planet Venus was named after the ▶ Roman goddess of beauty and love.

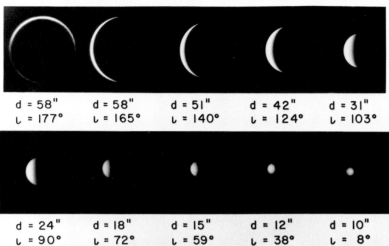

VENUS – ANGULAR DIAMETER VERSUS PHASE ANGLE

| d = 58" | d = 58" | d = 51" | d = 42" | d = 31" |
| ι = 177° | ι = 165° | ι = 140° | ι = 124° | ι = 103° |

| d = 24" | d = 18" | d = 15" | d = 12" | d = 10" |
| ι = 90° | ι = 72° | ι = 59° | ι = 38° | ι = 8° |

the morning, Venus is some-times called the morning star. It is called the evening star when seen at night.

In 1610, an Italian **astrono-mer** named Galileo Galilei (1564–1642) used a **telescope** to study Venus. He saw that Venus goes through phases,

▲ *At different times, we see Venus as a thin curve (upper left), a thick curve (upper right), a half-circle (lower left), or a full-circle (lower right).*

▸ *Galileo was the first person to use a telescope to study Venus.*

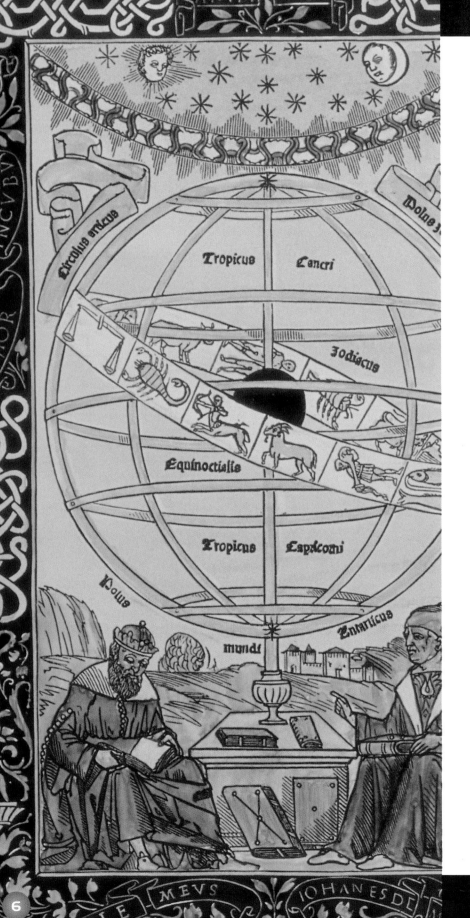

much like our Moon. This means that Venus does not always look like a round circle. Sometimes it is shaped like a half-circle or a thin curve. Venus seems to change shape because we only see part of the sunlit side of Venus at one time.

The phases of Venus solved a problem among astronomers. The Greek astronomer Ptolemy and others thought Earth was the center of the **solar system**. The Polish astronomer Nicolaus Copernicus and others thought that the Sun was

◄ *Ptolemy (2nd century A.D.) and others thought that Earth was the center of the solar system. They believed that the planets and stars circled around Earth.*

the center. The fact that Venus goes through phases proved that the Sun is the center of the solar system.

Venus is often the closest planet to Earth. For a long time, Venus was called Earth's sister planet. Both planets are rocky and are almost the same size. But Venus and Earth are quite different. People could not live on Venus. There is no water on Venus, and the air would poison people. Also, many hot **volcanoes** are found on the surface of Venus.

◀ *Copernicus (1473–1543) studied the movements and phases of Venus and the other planets. He thought that the Sun was the center of the solar system.*

Looking at the Way Venus Moves

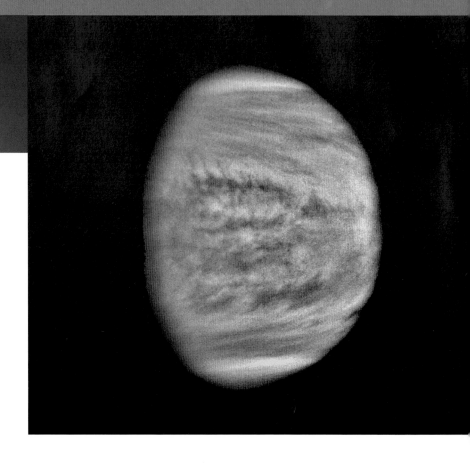

★ Venus travels around the Sun, or revolves, in a path called an orbit. It takes Venus one Venus-year, or about 225 Earth-days, to go around the Sun. It takes Earth one Earth year, or 365 Earth-days, to go around the Sun.

Venus also spins, or rotates, as it travels around the Sun. One rotation is one day on Venus. The rotation of Venus is different from the other planets. Venus spins very slowly. A day on Venus lasts for 243 Earth-days. So, on Venus, one day lasts longer than one year! Venus also spins in the opposite direction from most of the other planets. If you could stand on Venus, you would see the Sun rise in the west and set in the east.

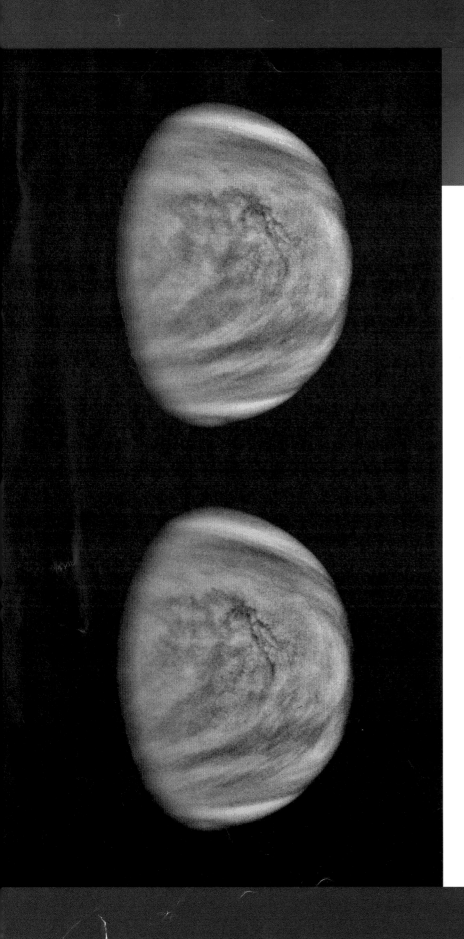

Looking Through Venus

✦ Mercury, Venus, Earth, and Mars are called rocky planets. This is because they are made mostly of iron and rock. Venus and the other rocky planets have round **cores** in their centers made of iron. A layer called the mantle is around the core. It is made of hot liquid. The mantle is covered by a thin rocky crust.

Venus has a thick, cloudy atmosphere. A planet's atmosphere is made up of the gases

◀ *Venus's thick clouds move very quickly. These three pictures were taken over three days. Can you see how the clouds change from day to day?*

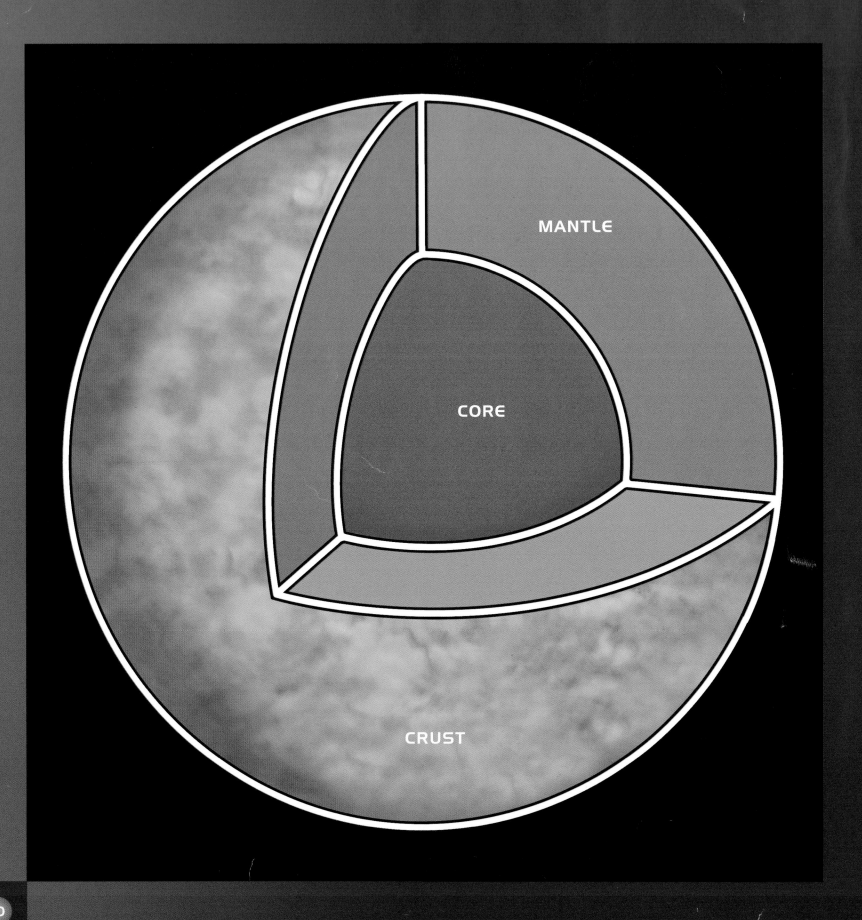

around it. The Sun's light bounces off the clouds. This makes Venus look bright to people on Earth. But the clouds are so thick that we can't see the surface of Venus. Astronomers need to use other tools, such as radar, to "look" under the clouds. Radar bounces radio signals off the planet. These signals tell us which areas of Venus are flat and which are bumpy.

Venus has the thickest atmosphere of any planet. The atmosphere is so thick that it puts a lot of pressure on the planet. It is made mostly of carbon dioxide and nitrogen. Carbon dioxide is a gas that is deadly to people. The atmosphere is also filled with tiny drops of sulfuric acid, another deadly substance.

The clouds in the upper part of the atmosphere whip around the planet at very high speeds. They travel about 215 miles (346 kilometers) per hour. It takes these clouds only four days to travel around the planet. The winds near the surface are much slower—only about 4 miles (6.4 kilometers) per hour.

◀ *The iron core of Venus is surrounded by a layer called the mantle. This is covered by a thin crust of rock.*

Looking at the Surface of Venus

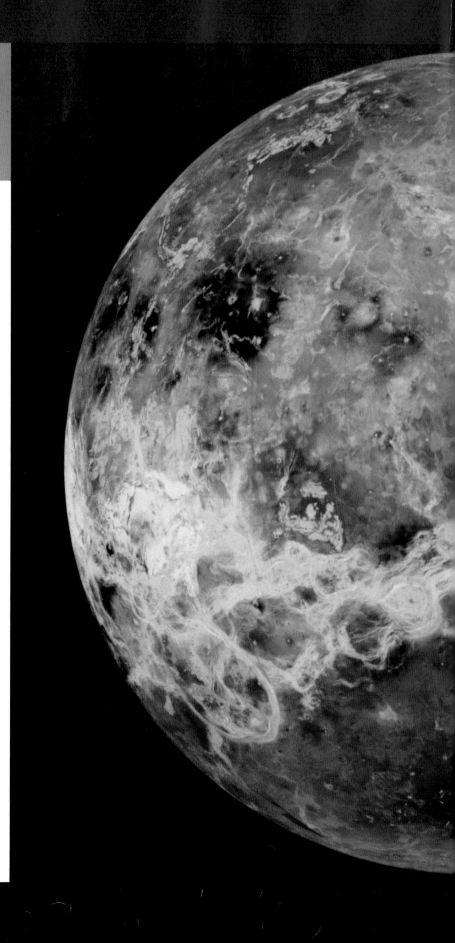

Its thick clouds make Venus the hottest planet in the solar system. Temperatures on the surface can rise to almost 900° Fahrenheit (518° Celsius). That is hot enough to melt the metal lead. This is because Venus acts like a giant greenhouse. A greenhouse is a building where people grow plants. It lets the heat of the Sun in, but doesn't let it out. So it gets very hot inside a greenhouse. On Venus, the clouds let the Sun's heat reach the surface. But then the

Scientists used radar to look through ▶
Venus's clouds and take this "picture" of the surface.

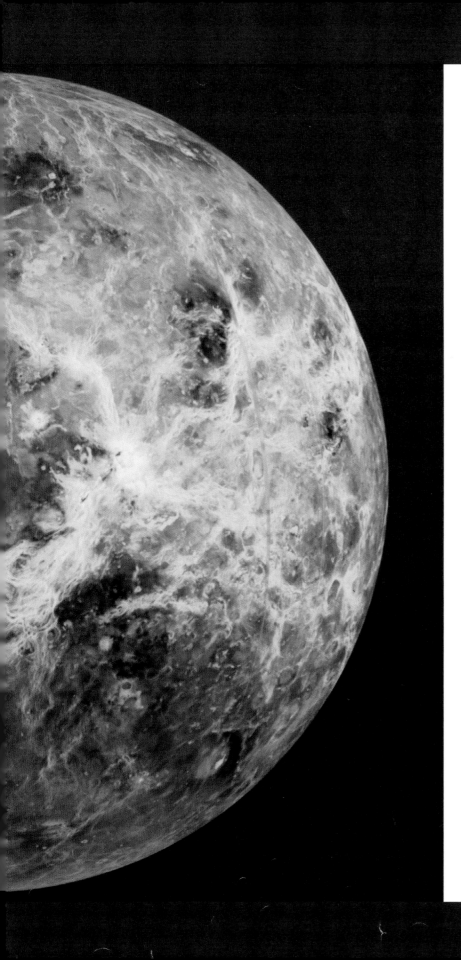

clouds trap the heat and stop it from going out. So the surface gets very warm. This is called the greenhouse effect.

The surface of Venus was made long ago by volcanoes. Volcanoes are mountains that shoot out a hot liquid called lava. The volcanoes on Venus once spread lava over the land. This made many flat areas called plains. The volcanoes also created rivers of lava. When the lava cooled, it left behind tracks that are hundreds of miles long. Today, Venus has nearly 600 small, wide volcanoes and 150 tall volcanoes. Maxwell Montes is one of the largest.

Only a few **craters** can be seen on the surface. These were created when pieces of rock called meteorites crashed into the planet. Most meteorites burn up in Venus's atmosphere before they can land.

Some scientists have another idea why there are so few craters. They believe that the core of Venus sometimes gets hot enough to melt the outer crust. When the crust cools, it becomes solid again. The craters that were once on the surface disappear.

▸▸ *Each of these craters is more than 20 miles (32 km) wide.*

◂ *Maat Mons is a 5-mile (8-kilometer)-high volcano on Venus. The volcano spread lava (light-colored areas) over hundreds of miles of land.*

Looking at Venus from Space

Venus is very close to Earth. So astronomers have sent more than twenty spacecraft to study the planet.

The Soviet Union, now Russia, sent some very successful missions to Venus. *Venera 1* flew by Venus in 1961. In 1970, *Venera 7* became the first spacecraft to land on another planet and send back information to Earth. It sent back information for twenty-three minutes before it was crushed by the

Mariner 10 *flew by Venus on its way to* ▶ *Mercury in 1974.*

pressure of Venus's atmosphere. Then, in 1975, *Venera 9* became the first spacecraft to send back pictures of the surface.

The United States also sent missions to Venus. *Mariner 2* in 1962, *Mariner 5* in 1967, and *Mariner 10* in 1974 all flew by Venus. Then, in 1978, the United States launched *Pioneer Venus*. One part of the spacecraft orbited around the planet. It also dropped four **probes** into the atmosphere in four different places. The

The Soviet spacecraft Venera 13 *landed on* ▲ *Venus in 1982. You can see part of the spacecraft in the lower left corner of the picture.*

The Pioneer Venus *orbiter studied Venus* ▶▶ *from 1980 until 1992. Then it ran out of fuel and crashed into the planet.*

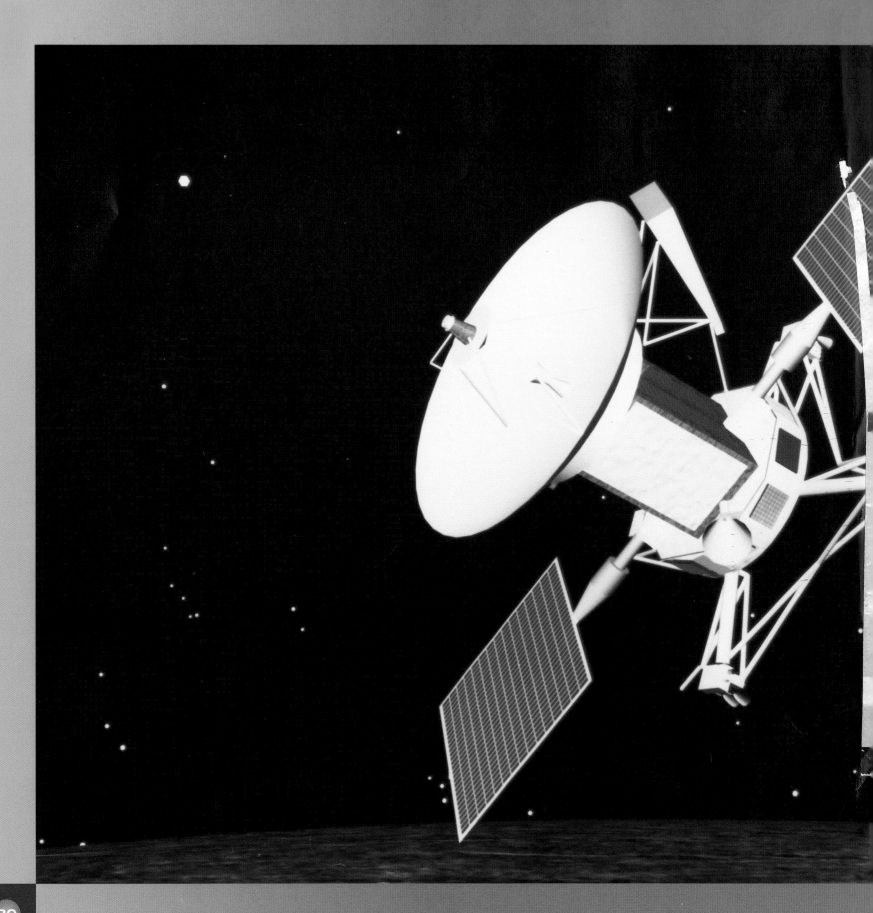

probes gathered information as they fell toward the surface.

The Soviets sent *Venera 15* and *16* in 1984. These were the first spacecraft to use radar in space. They sent back very clear pictures of the surface. They showed us landforms that had always been hidden by Venus's thick clouds.

Magellan was one of the most successful missions to Venus. It was named after a Portuguese explorer from the sixteenth century. Ferdinand Magellan was the first person to lead a trip around Earth.

◄ *The spacecraft* Magellan *orbited Venus from 1990 until 1994.*

Magellan was the first spacecraft launched by a **space shuttle**. The space shuttle *Atlantis* released it in 1989. *Magellan* used a new type of radar to study the surface. The radar gave astronomers a "picture" of almost all the planet's surface.

After four years, *Magellan* crashed into the planet. This was done on purpose. Scientists wanted to gather information on the atmosphere. The spacecraft sent back information about Venus's clouds as it fell to the surface.

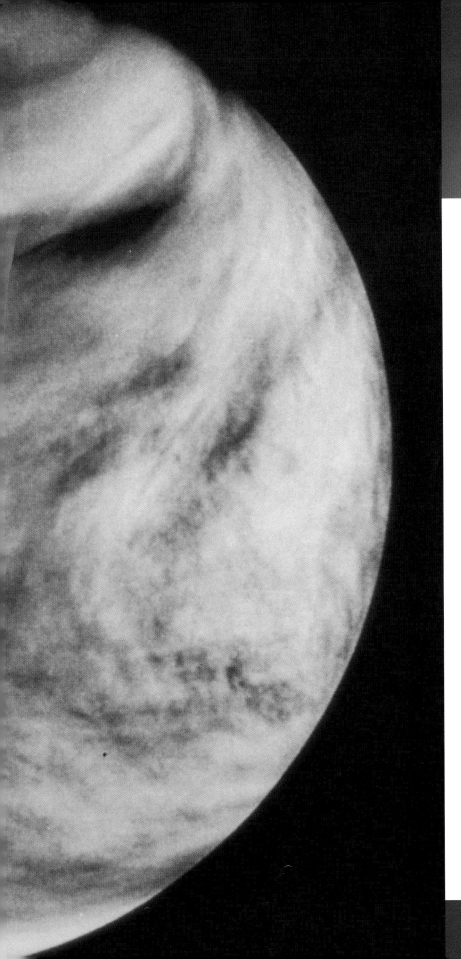

Looking to the Future

Galileo was the last space-craft to fly by Venus. In 1990, it passed Venus on its way to Jupiter. Another spacecraft will fly by Venus on its way to Mercury in 2005.

The information from *Magellan* and other missions has given astronomers enough material to study for a very long time. But scientists still have many questions about Venus. They want to know more about the planet's thick atmosphere, its great

◀ *Scientists still have many questions about Venus.*

heat, and its unusual rotation. They are also very curious about its volcanoes. On Earth, most volcanoes are found near the edges of plates—the moving pieces of Earth's crust. But on Venus, the crust does not move. Volcanoes are found all over the surface.

Venus and Earth are similar in size and distance from the Sun. So scientists wonder why Venus's atmosphere and surface are so different from Earth's. By studying Venus, scientists will try to figure out why Earth has life, and why Venus is hot and deadly to people.

◀ *Venus and Earth (seen at left from space) are sometimes called sister planets. But they are different in many ways.*

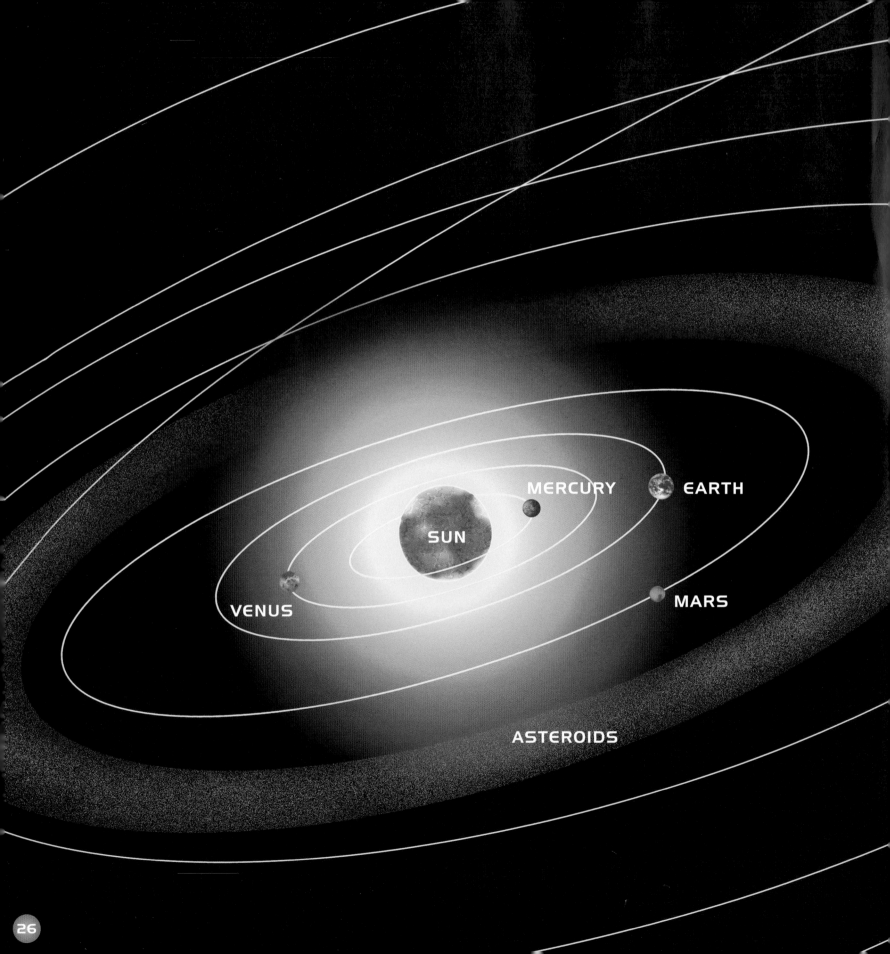

JUPITER

URANUS

SATURN

NEPTUNE

PLUTO

Glossary

astronomer—someone who studies space

cores—the centers of planets

craters—bowl-shaped landforms created by meteorites crashing into a planet

probes—parts of a spacecraft that drop to the surface of planets

radar—an instrument that bounces radio signals off an object to "see" what it looks like

solar system—a group of objects in space including the Sun, planets, moons, asteroids, comets, and meteoroids

space shuttle—a spacecraft that carries astronauts who work in space and returns to Earth when its mission is complete

telescope—a tool astronomers use to make objects look closer

volcanoes—mountains that may erupt with lava, or hot liquid rock

A Venus Flyby

Venus is the fourth smallest planet and the second planet from the Sun.

If you weighed 75 pounds (34 kilograms) on Earth, you would weigh 68 pounds (31 kilograms) on Venus.

Average distance from the Sun: 67 million miles (108 million km)

Distance from Earth: 24.7 million miles (41.4 million kilometers) to 160 million miles (257 million kilometers)

Diameter: 7,520 miles (12,104 kilometers)

Number of times Venus would fit inside Earth: 1

Did You Know?

- Venus's atmosphere puts so much pressure on the planet's surface that spacecraft landing there are crushed within a few minutes.

- Venus is hotter than Mercury, the closest planet to the Sun.

- The surface of Venus is hot enough to melt some kinds of metal.

- Venus has the longest "day" of any planet. It takes 243 Earth-days to rotate.

- Important missions to Venus include *Mariner 2, Venera 7, Mariner 10, Venera 9, Pioneer Venus,* and *Magellan.*

- On one mission to Venus, the spacecraft *Magellan* sent back more information than scientists had gathered in all the previous missions to all the planets.

- The same side of Venus faces Earth every time Venus passes Earth in its orbit.

- Venus's orbit is the most circular of all the planets.

- Venus has some high areas of land, like continents found on Earth.

Time it takes to circle around Sun (one Venus year) : 224.7 Earth-days

Time it takes to rotate (one Venus day) : 243 Earth-days

Structure: core (iron)
mantle (liquid rock)
crust (solid rock)

Temperature: 867° Fahrenheit (464° Celsius)

Atmosphere: carbon dioxide, nitrogen

Atmospheric pressure (Earth=1.0) : 92

Moons: 0

Rings: 0

Want to Know More?

AT THE LIBRARY

Asimov, Isaac. *Earth's Twin?: The Planet Venus*. Milwaukee: Gareth Stevens, 1996.

Brimner, Larry D. *Venus*. Danbury, Conn.: Children's Press, 1998.

Kipp, Steven L. *Venus*. Mankato, Minn.: Bridgestone Books, 2000.

Mitton, Jacqueline and Simon Mitton. *Scholastic Encyclopedia of Space*. New York: Scholastic Reference, 1998.

ON THE WEB

Exploring the Planets: Venus
http://www.nasm.edu/ceps/etp/venus/
For more information about Venus

The Nine Planets: Venus
http://www.seds.org/nineplanets/ nineplanets/venus.html
For a multimedia tour of Venus

Solar System Exploration: Missions to Venus
http://sse.jpl.nasa.gov/missions/ venus_missns/venus-m2.html
For more information about important NASA missions to Earth's sister planet

Space Kids
http://spacekids.hq.nasa.gov
NASA's space science site designed just for kids

Space.com
http://www.space.com
For the latest news about everything to do with space

Star Date Online: Venus
http://www.stardate.org/resources/ssguide/ venus.html
For an overview of Venus and hints on where it can be seen in the sky

Welcome to the Planets: Venus
http://pds.jpl.nasa.gov/planets/choices/ venus1.htm
For pictures and information about Venus and some of its most important surface features

THROUGH THE MAIL

Goddard Space Flight Center
Code 130, Public Affairs Office
Greenbelt, MD 20771
To learn more about space
exploration

Jet Propulsion Laboratory
4800 Oak Grove Drive
Pasadena, CA 91109
To learn more about the
spacecraft missions

Lunar and Planetary Institute
3600 Bay Area Boulevard
Houston, TX 77058
To learn more about Venus
and other planets

Space Science Division
NASA Ames Research Center
Moffet Field, CA 94035
To learn more about Venus and
solar system exploration

ON THE ROAD

**Adler Planetarium and
Astronomy Museum**
1300 S. Lake Shore Drive
Chicago, IL 60605-2403
312/922-STAR
Visit the oldest planetarium in
the Western Hemisphere

**_Exploring the Planets_ and
Where Next Columbus?**
National Air and Space Museum
7th and Independence Avenue, S.W.
Washington, DC 20560
202/357-2700
Learn more about the solar system
at this museum exhibit

**Rose Center for Earth and
Space/Hayden Planetarium**
Central Park West at 79th Street
New York, NY 10024-5192
212/769-5100
Visit this new planetarium and learn
more about the planets

UCO/Lick Observatory
University of California
Santa Cruz, CA 95064
408/274-5061
See the telescope that was used
to discover the first planets outside
our solar system

Index

◄ **About the Author:** *Dana Meachen Rau loves to study space. Her office walls are covered with pictures of planets, astronauts, and spacecraft. She also likes to look up at the sky with her telescope and write poems about what she sees. Ms. Rau is the author of more than sixty books for children, including nonfiction, biographies, storybooks, and early readers. She lives in Farmington, Connecticut, with her husband, Chris, and children, Charlie and Allison.*